HELP WANTED

An A to Z Guide to Cope with the Ups and Downs of the Job Search

KAREN LITZINGER, MA, LPC

Help Wanted An A to Z Guide to Cope with the Ups and Downs of the Job Search/Karen Litzinger, MA, LPC — 1st ed.

Paperback ISBN: 978-1-7377600-0-9

CONTENTS

INTRODUCTION

You'll find endless advice in hundreds of books and blogs about how to choose the ideal career and successfully land a job. That kind of counseling and coaching is what I've done my entire career.

But what about the angst, doubts, and darkness that often come during the process of using all of these strategies? Less attention goes to helping with the roller coaster of emotions during typical career coaching. Negative feelings can arise whether you are newly looking for a job while employed or struggling with long-term unemployment and job search burnout. Being aware of these normal feelings can help prevent job search depression and anxiety that may come as time goes on. *Help Wanted* is here to provide the help you want or need, whether for now or the future.

The book was written just before the COVID era, so naturally networking meetings referenced may be virtual or in-person. I hope that you will find comfort, support, and insight through the ups and downs of your job search.

Karen Litzinger

THE STORY BEHIND THE BOOK

The inspiration for and the many details in this book were given to me as if out of the blue, during a meditation at a spiritual retreat. I resurrected it two years later during a conference for career counselors. The speaker took us through an exercise as if we were clients. In looking at my patterns of interests, I became certain this project was mine to complete.

In retrospect, many experiences led me to this vision.

As a career counselor co-facilitating a job seekers support group, I witnessed the power of the emotional side of job hunting. I was working alongside a psychotherapist at a local agency. We gave no resume advice, no networking help; instead, we just listened and honored each client's journey and struggle. Our participants emerged from this process calmer, less worried, and more hopeful about their journey.

A couple of years after this, a struggling client replied to an email newsletter of mine asking if I had any words of encouragement. Grasping for help to supplement my own awkward words, I scoured the Internet to find resources on maintaining hope during the job search. I came up with only a few quotes.

My personal life also paved the way for this vision. In junior high school, I wrote prayers. As a senior in high school, I collected quotes for daily public service announcements.

As an adult, I bought or gave as gifts dozens of meditation and inspiration books helping everyone from worriers, to teens, to new mothers, to widows.

Despite all the books of meditation and inspiration, despite all the "how-to" material on job hunting, I realized there was a gap I needed to fill. As a career counselor, I felt this was my project to offer to society, my calling.

HOW TO USE THIS BOOK
AND BEYOND

The topics in this book represent a wide range of emotions and issues that many feel on the roller coaster ride of a job search.

Browse the A to Z topic list and see what speaks to you. Alternatively, open the book randomly, and you may find just what you need at the moment. Some topics may be more relevant to you than others. Use what resonates. Parts of the book may feel supportive and others may challenge your thinking. Allow openness.

All readings end with an affirmation that is rooted in cognitive behavior psychology. The premise is that our thoughts create feelings that affect our behavior. This technique can be used to reframe negative self-talk you may find yourself saying during your job search. Start with noticing. Then say something like, "Stop...that is a negative, unhelpful thought." Treat yourself kindly and try not to judge yourself. Come from an observer's point of view. Question or dispute any catastrophizing or generalizing you may have done; then find a more helpful, believable statement to say to yourself that makes you feel better. I hope these many examples of affirmations can help you be your own coach.

Another style of affirmation is related to the law of attraction. The premise is that you have the power to manifest what you state, e.g., "My ideal job offer is on its way."

Some psychological and spiritual experts say you must still believe with feeling in the affirmation statement for the outcome to come about.

Affirmations in this book may stretch you. Try the statement first, then reword it as you wish.

Experiment with what works for you to support yourself beyond job search strategy and technique. Emotional support strategies may include meditation, prayer, visualization, inspirational reading, support groups, job clubs, career or personal counseling, or perhaps these readings and affirmations.

You have more choice and power than you realize to create a happy and successful career.

"Life is 10 percent what you make it, and 90 percent how you take it."

Irving Berlin

ACCEPTANCE

Whether or not you accept what you are unable to change can mean peace or angst; moving forward or being stuck.

The sooner you make peace with a job loss or rejection, the sooner you can put energy into moving forward. Sometimes it's also hard to accept parts of the job search that are typically necessary, like networking. You may face challenges you can't change, like the job market, lack of experience, or age. You can, however, accept dead ends and change your goal, gain new skills, or even update your wardrobe.

Self-acceptance is another quality that can help a job search. Accept limitations while celebrating who you uniquely are and what you can offer. Another part of self-acceptance is not beating yourself up for past choices or difficulties. Take stock of what you learned from those experiences, change what you can, and use your energy to move forward.

I accept my past and present and move forward.

"What else does anxiety about the future bring you but sorrow upon sorrow?"

Thomas à Kempis

ANXIETY

Anxiety is a natural response to fear about the future. Perhaps you are worrying whether a new job will be worse than your current job. After all, even if you don't like parts of it, at least it is a known quantity. If you're in between jobs, the worry can be about money or how long it will take to land a new position. Anxiety is also a common feeling before or during interviews.

Even if worry and anxiety are understandable feelings, they can be paralyzing. This takes energy away from the present and from moving forward in a positive direction.

The first step is to be aware when you are in the grip of anxiety. Consider recognizing it with a non-judgmental, "Oh, there you are again" thought. Then take a slow breath or two, being aware of the sensations in your body as a way of grounding. Consciously breathing for just one minute can loosen the hold of anxiety. Try to talk to yourself as a dear friend might, such as, "You don't have control over the future. Just try to do what you can in this moment."

I take a conscious breath, coming back to the present moment, allowing the process to unfold.

"Stand up to your obstacles and do something about them. You will find that they haven't half the strength you think they have."

Norman Vincent Peale

BARRIERS

Whether real or imagined, a barrier can be a block in your job search that likely needs to be addressed.

Barriers can be emotional or physical. Some emotional issues may be anger about the past, anxiety over networking, or low confidence. More tangible obstacles may be age, lack of experience, overqualification, or a tight job market in your field.

First, be aware of what barriers might be holding you back. Taking action is the second step. For emotional barriers, learn new coping skills and tools to process feelings, including through counseling. Learning new career strategies can sometimes reduce anxiety and increase confidence as well.

More tangible career barriers may require some choices, like taking a computer class to dispel ageism, volunteering to gain work experience, communicating and accepting a lower salary if not breaking through, or shifting careers if the market is too tight. In many cases, networking or persuasive communication strategies can help get around an obstacle. Sometimes negative beliefs make the barrier even bigger than it is.

I recognize and take some action to offset barriers.

"It's not what you look at that matters, it's what you see."

Henry David Thoreau

BELIEFS

What we believe about ourselves and the job search can affect outcomes. Our thoughts and beliefs affect our feelings, which affect our behavior.

For example, if you say to yourself, "I'll never get a good job," then you'll typically have feelings of hopelessness. These feelings may bring about behaviors, such as procrastinating on that networking email or pulling the covers over your head in the morning.

One strategy that works for some is a positive affirmation, such as, "I trust I'll get the ideal job soon." If an affirmation is not believable, it might not result in helpful feelings or behaviors. An alternative is to dispute the negative belief with something realistic that makes you feel a bit better. For example, you might affirm, "Although I haven't found a job yet that suits me, I remind myself that I've had fine jobs in the past." This could shift feelings to hope and then shift behaviors to the next step of productive action.

I stay aware of negative
self-talk and beliefs and
reframe them.

"If you are insecure, guess what? The rest of the world is, too. Do not overestimate the competition and underestimate yourself. You are better than you think."

T. Harv Eker

CONFIDENCE

A job search can chip away at confidence, one rejection or unanswered email at a time. This happens to even the most accomplished people. Remember that this is simply one slice of your entire life.

Review successes that help boost your confidence as you move through the job search and interviews. Remind yourself of past accomplishments, whether they were on a past job, in the community, or for your family. Review positive performance evaluations or nice notes of any kind. Beyond reading or thinking, put yourself back in that positive time and space and actually feel the good feelings. Better yet, visualize a future job search circumstance such as a networking meeting or job interview right after experiencing the positive recollections. Another technique is to write a letter to yourself as if you were a friend or past colleague reminding you of the best of yourself.

And if you can't summon past feelings of confidence, then take on playing a role of "acting as if" you are confident, even if you don't feel that way right now.

> I remember the best of me
> to boost my confidence.

"Life shrinks or expands in proportion to one's courage."

Anais Nin

COURAGE

Sometimes it takes courage just to get out of bed in the morning to face the job search if things have not been going well. Sometimes courage is needed to even imagine leaving a job with real or perceived security to explore greater happiness. Courage must be summoned to take the next step, whether that is to make a networking request, call a career counselor, or follow up on an application. A single step is the key. Make that cup of coffee, turn on the computer, look up a phone number or email address. Think baby step. The next steps may likely be easier.

We can ask ourselves, "What's the worst that can happen?" Sure, there may be a rejection or disappointment, but we won't know until we try. Ask, "How will I feel if I don't try?" Think beyond right now, realizing that procrastination only gives short-term relief. How will I feel tomorrow or next week? Sometimes fear and negative self-talk make things worse than the real thing.

I rise above fear and
take a next step.

"Do not let your difficulties fill you with anxiety, after all it is only in the darkest nights that stars shine more brightly."

Imam Ali bin Abi Talib

DARKNESS

If we didn't have darkness we couldn't experience and appreciate light. Of course, we don't want to stay in the darkness that may come with some aspects of career transition, nor would we wish it on anyone. Yet it is an understandable reality. Embrace darkness as a visitor who will eventually leave. Perhaps even ask powerful questions such as, "What can I learn from you?" or "How can I lessen your impact?" Listen quietly.

Often energy can be shifted by taking a small step of action. You could send an email or hit the apply button on a vacancy. Equally as important are steps for self-care, such as exercising, reading something inspirational, listening to a favorite song, or taking a warm bath. Take a small step to bring light to someone, even if it's simply a caring word to a cashier or a thank-you note for a networking meeting. Your sharing light may lift your darkness.

If you are in that dark space too long, then consider professional assistance to help shift your heart, mind, and spirit to enable continued healing and career progress. Perhaps your darkness will add depth to who you are and allow you to better help others, whether in your career or personal life.

I accept darkness as part of the
human condition and take steps
to move forward.

"I have learned over the years that when one's mind is made up, this diminishes fear."

Rosa Parks

DECISIONS

Should I change careers? Should I apply for this job? Should I follow up one more time? Should I accept this offer or try for something better? So many big and little decisions come up in a job search.

It can be helpful to remember there are no absolute right or wrong choices, although some may be better than others. Recognizing that a choice may lead to another fork in the road, rather than the final destination, can help lift the enormity and stress. Perfection and fear can sometimes lead to paralysis, missed opportunities, and disappointment. Not making a decision is also a decision.

When faced with a decision, try to remember your overall goal and priorities. Consider the decision from a balanced perspective of logic and information as well as your intuition and gut feeling. Visualize yourself in the different options and pay attention to the physical sensations in your body as well as your emotions. Which choice brings relief? Which choice brings regret? Trust, take action, and let go.

I use both information and
intuition as I make decisions.

"I've come to trust not that events will always unfold exactly as I want, but that I will be fine either way."

Marianne Williamson

DISAPPOINTMENT

Dashed hopes are typically part of the job search. You may have received very positive feedback from the interviewers, yet they chose to hire someone else. You may have been in communication about a lead for months, and then there was a hiring freeze.

When expectations aren't met, negative thoughts can invade. Acknowledge and allow your feelings, and then move forward. Calm yourself through a walk or nap or distract yourself through a movie or book. Counter low energy through exercise or upbeat music.

On a deeper level, take inventory. What did you learn and what can you do differently in the future? A common mistake of job seekers is to stop or slow other efforts when a promising lead is at hand. Try to transform your perspective. For example, was there a red flag you were ignoring, such that not getting the position may be positive after all? View this as a temporary situation. Try not to demand perfection by torturing yourself about what you could have done differently. You're only human. And so are the recruiters.

I can cope and move forward
from disappointment.

"*Your emotions are the slaves to your thoughts, and you are the slave to your emotions.*"

Elizabeth Gilbert

EMOTIONS

The job search can bring a roller coaster of emotions. It may begin with confusion about goals or anger about a past or current job. A great fitting job lead can bring hope, and an interview can bring excitement or fear. Waiting to hear back after interviews and emails can bring frustration. Over time, lack of job search success and financial concerns can bring depression or despair. Then there may be another lead and another round on the roller coaster.

Recognize that all of these emotions are normal and natural for job seekers. Allow yourself to fully feel your emotions in a safe way. Negative emotions that are bottled up often seep out during an interview or are the reason for not getting positive responses to networking requests.

So punch a pillow, write in a journal, or share with a select group of trusted friends or support group. Consider meeting with a career counselor or therapist. Keep taking care of yourself physically, emotionally, and spiritually; and hang on for the ride.

I take care of myself and stay grounded through the ups and downs.

"It really is an endurance race."

Henry Ford

ENDURANCE

A job search can take longer than you expect. Endurance is the ability to sustain a stressful effort. Since you don't know how long your job search will take, it's good to proactively build endurance like an athlete. Even if you are well into your search, there are practices and exercises to do to increase your mental stamina.

Consistency is the key in any performance training. Besides a routine of job search activities, create a routine of emotional self-care practices. Consider a morning warm-up such as an affirmation or prayer upon waking. Cool down your day with a gratitude list, meditation, or inspirational reading. Stay disciplined through the day by monitoring your thoughts to counter negativity. Develop patience with yourself and others. Like athletes, create a proactive plan to counter setbacks, like job rejections, so you don't spiral down. Techniques to recenter could be saying a phrase like, "All will be well," playing a song like, "I Will Survive," or doing 30 seconds of slow, deep breathing.

You have or can develop what you need to endure and succeed. Rather than passive suffering through hardship, take proactive steps to increase your endurance.

I will take steps to sustain myself in the job search.

"Courage is feeling fear, not getting rid of fear, and taking action in the face of fear."

Roy T. Bennett

FEAR

Our minds can run wild with worry about the future. *What if I can't find a job? What if this career change isn't feasible? What if I'm too old? What if I don't have enough experience?* While caught in the grip of fear, we can become paralyzed and depressed, and not in a good state to take action even if we could.

Beyond job search strategies, a person needs mental and emotional strategies to tame these gremlins. When your mind dives into doubt, challenge it. Ask yourself if you've known of anyone who has succeeded with similar circumstances, even if not personally. Seek out examples. Remind yourself of any evidence to balance negatives, such as job rejections, which are a natural part of the job search. Perhaps, ask yourself, "What's the worst that could happen?" or "What would I do if this doesn't work out?" Shining light on fear may reduce its control. Remind yourself of past successes and visually relive them, bringing forth the positive emotions of the time.

Then take an action step that can loosen fear's grip. Seek professional assistance if you feel too stuck, or if your mind tortures you rather than helps you. In the meantime, be gentle with yourself.

I shine light on my fears and
loosen their grip.

"My success, part of it certainly, is that I have focused in on a few things."

Bill Gates

FOCUS

Sometimes it's hard to know what you want or what to do. Focus is a key element in both career happiness and job search success. Feeling or thinking, "I just need a job" or "I'm flexible" can show desperation or confusion.

When thoughts, feelings, and choices are spinning in your head, the result is usually spinning your wheels. Find career tools or a career counselor to help you through the process. Then listen to your inner guidance. You may need to let go of a choice or dream to move forward. You can later revisit options in some fashion, whether through work, a hobby, or a retirement job.

Making clear decisions about your job targets can allow you to move forward more effectively in your search. Staying focused on job search activities can be challenging too. Concentrate your energy on the most valuable techniques rather than just keeping busy. Discipline and routine can help with distractions yet should be balanced with breaks and self-care.

I focus my choices and time as I move forward with my search.

"Let us rise up and be thankful, for if we didn't learn a lot today, at least we learned a little, and if we didn't learn a little, at least we didn't get sick, and if we got sick, at least we didn't die; so, let us all be thankful."

−Buddha

GRATITUDE

You may wonder, "How can I be thinking about gratitude when I'm in a cloud of career confusion or buried in rejections?" Gratitude is a coping tool during dark times, helping shift perspective. When we focus on lack, it creates negative energy that can paralyze our actions and repel people who may be able to help us.

Each day look for positive things: a beautiful sunset, a favorite food, an email from a friend, or a special moment with your child or pet. Maybe there are elements about your search process you can be grateful for, such as an email reply, a job prospect, or a networking meeting, even if only five minutes of it was helpful. Perhaps there is even something to be grateful for in the midst of the search itself, whether getting to spend more time with family due to a job loss or recognizing your courage to explore a new direction.

Consider starting a gratitude journal and writing down five short bullets about what you are grateful for each night before you go to bed. If you're stuck, then write down that you have a bed to sleep in or a roof over your head. Think of one thing you are grateful for before getting out of bed, and that can change the course of your day.

Each day I notice things and people for whom I am grateful.

"You cannot teach a man anything; you can only help him find it within himself."

–Galileo Galilei

GUIDANCE

There are so many sources of external guidance in the career search. Perhaps you've heard from friends or family, "Why don't you look into this career or that job vacancy?" You may get a different opinion on your resume from every person you ask. People naturally give their advice from their own perspectives and values. While it can be helpful to hear some outside opinions, especially from career coaches, human resources professionals, or people in your field, in the end, everything is your decision.

Go inside for your inner wisdom. Allow that still, small voice to emerge through meditation, prayer or simply sitting in silence. You may not want to pursue a certain vacancy or job search strategy after all; honoring your choice may be wise since you may not bring enough positive energy to a position or technique you cannot get excited about. Find another option, another strategy, one that feels better. On the other hand, do examine if fear or procrastination may be influencing your path, and use strategies to help with these barriers. Internal thoughts about not making a networking call or going back to bed could be more about avoidance than guidance, unless you are burned out from multiple, 40-hour job search weeks and need to take a reasonable break.

In the end, your inner guidance is what will likely bring you more peace and happiness, and therefore, more success.

I listen to and honor
my inner guidance.

"*The secret of health for both mind and body is not to mourn for the past, not to worry about the future, or not to anticipate troubles, but to live the present moment wisely and earnestly.*"

Buddha

HEALING

Sometimes events from the past take a toll, whether it was how your last job ended, how you were treated on the job, or rejections in the job search. Recognize, honor and process any painful feelings so they don't come out in ways that do not benefit you. Past hurts held onto can often seep out in communication and attitude without realizing it.

We can heal past hurts in many ways. Allowing tears to flow is healing. Expressing anger by hitting a pillow or bed is another approach. A good run or workout could be a helpful way to channel frustration or hurt. Some good yells in the car with the windows up and radio blasting can also be therapeutic; so can soft music, inspirational readings, prayer, meditation, or affirmations. Mentally reframing the event to move from blame to forgiveness is another helpful angle.

If you feel stuck in negative feelings, a professional counselor could help. Use whatever strategies work for healing. The goal is to let go and move forward. Your energy is needed to focus on the future.

I heal past hurts so I can let go
and move forward effectively.

"Hope is important, because it can make the present moment less difficult to bear. If we believe that tomorrow will be better, we can bear a hardship today."

Thich Nhat Hanh

HOPE

Some days or weeks it can feel like you've reached a wall you can't get around. Your applications are met with deafening silence or rejection, and you can't bear to reach out for one more networking meeting. You may be losing hope that the offer you are waiting for will ever come through. Sometimes you don't want to hope for the risk of being disappointed yet again.

Allow yourself to remember that you have survived dark times before. The human spirit is resilient even if you don't feel that way right now. There are indeed jobs being filled every day. Celebrate when others get jobs rather than asking, "Why not me?" Another's success means it can happen to you. Consider asking successful job seekers for insight and help.

Recall something good that happened in the job search last week or last month, no matter how small. Breathe and take your next baby step on the journey. Make it an easy one to help you gain some momentum and shift perspectives.

I allow space in my mind and spirit to believe I will get a job soon.

"Be yourself; everyone else is already taken."

Oscar Wilde

IDENTITY

Career is often intertwined with identity. When someone meets you at a social event, the first question is typically, "What do you do?" When you're between jobs, that question can make you want to crawl under a rock or isolate yourself. If you are exploring a career change for greater happiness, you can have a hard time seeing yourself doing something else, or you may have lost track of who you really are as you "perform" your job. If you are successful at a career, you may become entrenched in that identity, even if you are unhappy. Risk and change can be threatening, so it's natural to stay where you are comfortable, even though you may not be truly comfortable.

We are not our jobs; this is simply one part of life. Work can seem so significant because of the number of waking hours we spend there and because society places so much value on this role.

Remind yourself of the other roles in your life, whether a loving family member, loyal friend, helpful volunteer, avid learner, or spiritual traveler. You are valuable just because you are here on this planet.

I value and express who I am
in many ways.

"*I believe in intuitions and inspirations... I sometimes FEEL that I am right. I do not KNOW that I am.*"

Albert Einstein

INTUITION

Moments of "aha" and insights that feel "out of the blue" are often intuition showing up. Intuition might also be that uneasy feeling during an interview that is a red flag to a problem. It can be a hunch to contact a past colleague that results in perfect timing to learn of a vacancy.

Intuition is the way the brain stores, processes, and retrieves information on the subconscious level. It's the still, small voice within that feels more like deeper knowing than the reactive chatter of fear, negativity, and debate. Intuition comes to us more from feeling and body sensations than through thinking. It can support and balance the analytical side of decision-making.

Accessing intuition can be as simple as taking a break from what is at hand. Go for a walk or engage in a creative project. Do something repetitive, like chopping carrots, to calm the cognitive side of your brain and open intuition. Developing intuition can also come through meditation, journaling, dreamwork, or simply asking a question and listening. Accessing intuition can reduce stress and increase confidence.

I pay attention to clues of inner knowing.

"You can't laugh and be afraid at the same time – of anything."

Stephen Colbert

JOKING

Perhaps you're thinking, "You must be joking!" about including a topic on joking in an inspirational career book. Looking for a job is no laughing matter...unless you want to stay sane.

With stress about career identity, finances, and rejections, joking and humor are important coping mechanisms. Humor can help us from getting overwhelmed or too scared. Laughter changes the body chemistry by releasing dopamine, the same neurotransmitter that creates drug-induced euphoria. A smile, even a fake one, releases endorphins that help lower stress levels.

Turn on a comedy, read a funny book, or watch silly cat videos. If you're adventurous, find a laughter club. Consider the strategy of creating your own humor by imagining extremes of your situation, such as arriving at an interview with a 100-page resume and nine nice colleagues who want to give in-person references. If you need help with humor, do an Internet search on "Job Search Humor" and find bloopers, like a cover letter mistake reading, "Here are my qualifications for you to overlook."

I can laugh or cry.
I choose laughter.

"Joy does not simply happen to us. We have to choose joy and keep choosing it every day."

Henri Nouwen

JOY

It may be hard to find joy in the job search or even see joy on the horizon in a new job. Yet each day we have a choice about how to see our life. We can be consumed by the negativity of job search fear or frustration, or we can allow some space to notice a sunset or a child's laughter. Brief moments of joy can be a respite from the work of finding work. Perhaps we can even stretch to find some joy by answering yes to a networking request or a nugget of wisdom someone shares.

We can, and sometimes must, create our own joy for the sake of our emotional health and for the well-being of those around us whose support we want and need. Experiencing moments of joy can also help a person to be a more desirable job candidate since employers may sense positivity.

So turn on a comedy, gaze at the clouds, listen to music, and hug a child.

I find moments of joy in my life
and am grateful.

"There are three ways to ultimate success: The first way is to be kind. The second way is to be kind. The third way is to be kind."

Fred Rogers

KINDNESS

Kindness softens our edges. Although we may feel most in need of kindness during the job search, we are well-served to extend it.

Sometimes we can feel we are being treated unkindly in the job search. We may be not hearing back in a timely way after an interview or from a networking lead. People have busy schedules and competing needs. Give them the benefit of the doubt, and you'll likely feel better. The alternative may be bitterness, which will not help in the job search.

Beyond the search, spread kindness wherever you can. Because of the stressful job search journey, you may know more than others the benefit of a smile, an encouraging word, or extra effort. Sharing kindness from your heart can help your soul and may even attract kindness towards you.

I extend kindness to others
as I would like to receive it.

"*Real knowledge is to know the extent of one's ignorance.*"

Confucious

KNOWLEDGE

You've got a good education and relevant experience and yet still no job. For interviews, you may be researching the employer thoroughly, yet you haven't landed the offer. Even when you think you have solid experience and are using good strategies, it can still take longer than expected to bring the job search to a successful conclusion.

Step back and look at the concept of knowledge in your job search. Ask yourself some probing questions. *Do I have enough training and experience, or do I need to take a course to brush up or volunteer to get recent experience? Am I honoring my strengths and interests or looking for things that aren't a fit? Am I getting lost in research and not spending enough time on action?*

You may be on track and simply need patience and time. Lack of knowledge or awareness can sometimes get in the way of progress. Reflection and new action may bring energy, confidence, and better results. Consider meeting with a trusted colleague for brainstorming, attending a professional association meeting for job market information, or meeting with a career counselor for mock interview feedback.

**I seek new insights
and try new actions.**

"We must let go of the life we have planned, so as to accept the one that is waiting for us."

Joseph Campbell

LETTING GO

We can get stuck in negative emotions during the search. Letting go gives a path forward. Sometimes a job transition is not your choice. You may have been "let go." Sometimes we're currently employed but in a poor career fit or toxic environment. Sometimes we feel treated unfairly in the job search process. It is natural to feel a range of emotions, including anger, frustration, and bitterness.

Feeling and expressing emotions in a healthy way is helpful and possibly even necessary to moving forward. Punch a pillow, write in a journal, hammer nails, see a counselor. Do whatever works for you. Moving through and letting go of negative emotions can lead to more acceptance and make room for hope and opportunity. Forgiving someone is more about helping you than the perceived offender.

If we do not let go of past hurts, they can subtly seep out as negative energy in networking meetings and job interviews despite our thinking we are projecting our best self.

I let go of past hurts so I can move forward authentically.

"Luck is what happens when preparation meets opportunity."

Seneca

LUCK

Why do others seem to get the lucky breaks, you may wonder? As the saying goes, you may feel down on your luck in this job search period. The definition of luck is success or failure apparently brought by chance rather than through one's actions. The word "apparently" leaves some room for wondering.

Can you create some luck in your life and job search? Rather than leave luck to random chance, try some new behaviors and thinking. Break routines and allow room in your schedule for synchronicity to happen. Try something new. Meet someone new. Expect lucky ideas and be on the lookout. Be observant of circumstances and surroundings. When you have a hunch or get an idea, write it down. Focus on positives even amid challenges. Help someone in need and you may notice gratitude for what you have.

Try to stay in the present moment rather than lost in your thoughts, since the present moment is where luck can occur.

I take action to create and notice serendipity.

"The meaning of life is whatever you ascribe it to be. Being alive is the meaning."

Joseph Campbell

MEANING

Career transitions can present opportunities to find meaning. The job search can be a chance to find a career with meaning and purpose. The process can also create self-understanding and growth.

If your current or past employment had negative aspects, finding meaning could include reflecting on what you want in your next position or work environment. Reflect on if there are any internal changes you need to make so the next chapter of your career can be better.

A job change, whether chosen or imposed, can be a crossroads to something better and more meaningful. A change may more fully tap into your talents and interests or be with an employer whose products, services, or values you believe in. Reflection and feedback can increase the chances of future career satisfaction.

I explore meaning to make
good choices.

"The thing that motivates me is a very common form of motivation. And that is, with other folks counting on me, it's so easy to be motivated."

Jeff Bezos

MOTIVATION

Sometimes you may want to turn off your computer and grab the remote as well as a carton of ice cream...or go back to bed. If you're putting 40+ hours into the search, you may be heading for burnout and actually do need to take a break to recharge. Choose time off deliberately, rather than the path of spontaneous indulgence and guilt.

Maintaining motivation over time in the job search can be a challenge. Acknowledging uncomfortable feelings in the search has its time and place; so does tolerating discomfort and doing hard things now to feel better later. Tell yourself, "I can do hard things" or "I will feel better if I get this done," and remind yourself when you rose to the occasion in the past. Reflect on an underlying reason that you want to move forward as a motivator, whether for money, pride, career satisfaction, or family obligation.

Other concrete strategies are trying something new; creating lists to track progress; and taking one small, easy step. Listening to a motivating talk or reading an inspirational blog can also give support.

I choose to take constructive action now to help me feel better later.

"It's no use saying, 'We are doing our best.' You have got to succeed in doing what is necessary."

Winston Churchill

NECESSARY

Some things are simply necessary for the job search, even if undesirable to do. A resume is a requirement, though it's not always read. Networking is essential to tap the hidden job market. The word unavoidable is a synonym for necessary; the "no's" that most people go through to get to the one "yes" are most likely unavoidable.

Needful is another much less common word for *necessary* and brings to mind the word *needy*, which is how you may feel during the job search. Realize that we all need help sometime in our lives. Try not to let pride get in the way of asking for or receiving help. Allow yourself to imagine how you would feel if someone asked you for reasonable help. Most people respond positively if circumstances allow; keep this in mind if you feel uncomfortable with a networking request.

Rise to the occasion to do what is necessary in the job search, even if you feel needy at times. Then, pay it forward to help someone else.

I motivate myself to do what is necessary for the job search.

"Normal is in the eye of the beholder."

Whoopi Goldberg

NORMAL

What used to feel normal may not be anymore. The job search can crush even a confident person. You may second guess your skills despite a record of success. You may wonder if you're bothering people despite good relationships. You may think you're boring despite interesting non-work experiences.

On the emotional side, you may wonder if what you are experiencing is normal. Most likely your feelings are part of the natural ups and downs of the search, but if in doubt, consider seeking professional counseling.

The job search itself is usually harder on a person than actually performing a job. Be gentle with yourself, especially if the new normal feels disconcerting. You will reclaim your best self at some point. This period is just one chapter in life's journey.

I remind myself of the best of
who I've been through my life.

"If you always do what you've always done, you'll always get what you've always got."

Jessie Potter

OPENNESS

Staying open to people and ideas can make your job search more interesting and successful. At the same time, being "open to any job" can show desperation. Find a balance between openness and proactive focus.

Stay open to meeting people even though you may feel vulnerable and less confident at points during the search. Beyond the success rates of networking, benefits include human connection and fostering curiosity. You never know what you might learn, even if it's your seventieth meeting. Valuable coincidences and synchronicity can come from openness and action.

Do what you need to do in clarifying your goals to move forward on a focused search while keeping open to new people and new ideas. Pay attention to what comes your way.

I am open to meeting new people and considering new ideas.

*"A wise man
will make more
opportunities than
he finds."*

Francis Bacon

OPPORTUNITY

A job vacancy is what may most come to mind with the word *opportunity*. A chance for a job or promotion is one of the standard definitions. Another definition is a set of circumstances favorable for the attainment of a goal. This perspective can sound like luck; at the same time, we can have some control over our circumstances no matter what the situation. We can create circumstances for opportunity to emerge.

Arranging a networking meeting is creating circumstances for an opportunity. Attending a job club meeting or a workshop in your field are other avenues. Less obvious ways to create circumstances for opportunities are to volunteer, attend social events, or ask a networking question when someone says, "How are you?"

Don't wait for opportunity to knock. Reach out to connect directly or even behind the scenes, such as through a LinkedIn interest group.

I take steps to create circumstances for opportunities.

"*Perseverance is failing 19 times and succeeding the 20th.*"

Julie Andrews

PERSISTENCE

It can be hard to keep going when you've submitted endless applications and had dozens of networking meetings, with no final success. Sometimes we do need to regroup and evaluate what we can do differently.

To get to that one offer, you may simply need to send out one more application or make one more call. Remind yourself that people do get jobs, even those with barriers to employment. Seek out people and stories that give you hope and energy to persist. Grit is a trait attributed to success.

Many inventors, writers, and dreamers were rejected or failed dozens or hundreds of times before getting their "yes." Among them are Walt Disney, Steven Spielberg, Dr. Suess, and J.K. Rowling. You are in good company. Keep at it. Try a new angle. Look for a good fit. Employers are looking to fill jobs. It only takes one. Then help someone else.

I persist with grit and
rise to the occasion.

"You may delay, but time will not, and lost time is never found again."

Benjamin Franklin

PROCRASTINATION

Tasks don't get any easier when you put them off. Actually tasks often get harder as the challenges become bigger in your head and the weight of guilt lays heavy on your shoulders. Household projects call to you, family matters capture your attention, everyday activities of living absorb your time. Often the issue is more lack of will, discipline, or motivation than lack of time.

Start with one small step. Record a half-hour on your calendar for a specific task. Make your goal an easy one. Rather than drafting the networking email you've been avoiding, maybe write down five goals for the week or organize your workplace.

Activity creates momentum, which can positively affect your energy. Challenge yourself next to take on a hard task rather than putting it off another day. Consider enlisting a check-in buddy to ask you weekly about goals and successes and perhaps offer support and encouragement. When you do deliberately take time off, enjoy it fully.

I recognize when I'm
procrastinating and take one
easy step to get unstuck.

"Positive attitudes qualify you for positive experiences."

Bryant McGill

QUALIFIED

Feeling qualified for a job but not being chosen is very frustrating. Sometimes we're not sure if we're qualified, which might cause us to not try for an opportunity. It can be painful to accept that getting a job isn't just about qualifications.

Employers are seeking that elusive chemistry, just as we do when we seek life partners. Can we blame them? After all, we are often spending more waking hours with coworkers than family. Accepting rather than resenting chemistry in the job search may open doors.

Although sometimes painful, we need to look closely at ourselves to see if we have the concrete and soft skills employers are seeking. Networking is almost always the best strategy to find an employer who fits or will take a chance on our unique style and skills. We all have something to offer that can be appreciated by an employer. Focusing on the positive will help you come across as a more qualified and desired candidate.

I remember and accept that job search success is about more than simply being qualified.

"Be curious, not judgmental."

Walt Whitman

QUESTIONING

You may be wondering if the job offer will ever arrive, if you're qualified enough, or if an obstacle you are facing can be overcome. Sometimes questioning can be resolved with factual information, and sometimes doubts and questions can be addressed with emotional strategies. In either case, curiosity can help shine a light on the path forward.

Related to possibly needing more facts, ask yourself the question, "What additional information might I need?" Perhaps research whether you need more experience, training, or new strategies. Read articles and ask good questions in networking meetings.

Related to emotions, try not to let your doubts win. Ask yourself the question, "Is this serving me?" Sometimes it is helpful to write down your doubts and questions rather than have them swirl in your head. If you get lost in self-doubt, say, "Stop, I'm not going down this road again." Avoid comparing yourself to others. Remind yourself that you are not a failure just because of setbacks.

I allow curiosity and learning to guide my questioning.

"Rest when you're weary. Refresh and renew yourself, your body, your mind, your spirit. Then get back to work."

Ralph Marston

RENEWAL

Finding the energy to keep going in the job search can be hard. We must find a way to renew our spirits and take the next step forward. Sometimes that may involve rest for the body, mind, and spirit, yet too much rest can lead to excuses and procrastination.

Sometimes we can be renewed by that which is around us if we pay attention and allow ourselves to be in the right frame of mind. Renewal can come from blossoming flowers in the springtime, sparkling fresh snow in the winter, or through an unexpected smile of a stranger. We remind ourselves that although trees look barren in the winter, they are still full of life, ready to come forth in the right time. Similarly, seeds of plants take time to peek through the soil and time to bear fruit.

Even if you are weary from what appear to be fruitless efforts in the job search, keep planting your seeds of effort. Plant one more resume, phone call, and networking meeting. Water them with positive energy, however hard to muster. Pay attention to your seedlings and follow up as needed. Prune negative interactions from your life that may choke your energy. Have faith that at the right time for the right job, your seeds of effort will be rewarded, and you will blossom with your new opportunity.

I remember that life can spring forth following barren times.

"It is during our darkest moments that we must focus to see the light."

Aristotle Onassis

REJECTION

While it is a common view that we have to go through many no's to get to a yes (whether job, relationship, or sales), it doesn't make it any easier. The "we've found someone who is a better match" reply (if you are lucky enough to hear back) can chip away at one's confidence and identity.

Try to remember that the employer is making a business decision and not rejecting you personally, or even saying you couldn't do the job. If the job wasn't a match from their perspective, you may not have enjoyed it or succeeded after all. Hold the vision that there is something better out there for you.

In the meantime, do your due diligence. Ask for feedback about your interviewing skills and what you can do to strengthen your candidacy for this type of position. Look inside to see if you truly think this path is a good fit. Look outside to see if this is a realistic goal. If another rejection comes your way, remind yourself that you are more than your career and have value beyond this search. Try to develop a thick skin and be kind to yourself. Remember, it only takes one yes.

I am gentle with myself when I experience rejection.

"You may have to fight a battle more than once to win it."

Margaret Thatcher

RESILIENCE

You might sometimes wonder if you're going to "bounce back" from your job loss, or perhaps you are struggling to regain your confidence from a dysfunctional work environment.

Resilience is a process of being able to adapt and move forward in the face of adversity or trauma. One still feels the emotion and distress yet brings forth thoughts and actions to cope.

Anyone can learn to develop resilience, though some may have more at hand based on circumstances and tendencies. A key strategy for resilience is creating a support system and accepting help, even simply a listening ear. Another angle is to focus on the situation as temporary, or even as an opportunity; you can't change the reality, but you can shift how you interpret it. Brainstorm what you can do or say to help you feel a bit better. Take action rather than wishing that the pain will go away.

I acknowledge the pain and do
something positive to cope.

*"Move and the way
will open."*

Zen proverb

STUCK

After significant job search efforts with no final result, you may feel stuck and wonder what you can do differently. At any point you may feel emotionally stuck with little motivation to take action.

Step back to see if something may be holding you back emotionally. Are there resentments from the past to let go of or a feeling of victimhood that is in your subconscious? Consider writing down or saying things out loud as if to a best friend you are trying to help. An additional emotional strategy is to assess the cost of inaction, such as in terms of self-esteem or time.

Another angle of getting unstuck is to adjust your strategy. Try something new. Meet someone new. Talk to someone for new ideas to consider, remembering you don't need to take that person's advice. Brainstorm ideas about what action to take and pick one that makes you feel good. Pierce resistance and create momentum by taking one very small step. Getting organized, creating a list, or making a timeline can also give a reset.

I uncover new perspectives
and try new strategies to
move forward.

"*Promise me you'll always remember: You're braver than you believe, and stronger than you seem, and smarter than you think.*"

A. A. Milne

SUPPORT

Even if we are independent spirits, the job search compels a need for support, both practical and emotional. Naturally, we need practical support through networking or perhaps a second set of eyes on a cover letter. We need emotional support from at least one or two trusted individuals to help weather job search storms.

Choose judiciously who to bear your job search troubles to as well as your aspirations. Even well-meaning family and friends can prematurely poke holes in dreams or offer too much advice. A spouse or partner can be too close to a situation because finances are involved.

Pick one to two people for venting since you may want others to see you in a good light for networking referrals. Seek out a job support group and/or career counselor. Process feelings through art or journaling. Consider a therapist for unconditional support and insight.

I recognize seeking support as a strength.

"The two most powerful warriors are patience and time."

Leo Tolstoy

TIME

Time can drag when you are waiting to hear from an employer. Time can feel like it's running out when you've been in the job search process for a while, facing impending financial pressures. Some days fly by productively, and some languish in misery.

We try to control time by all manner of goal-setting and time management techniques. While some strategy is important in the search for productivity, pause to reflect on the bigger picture. Allow yourself time for family, friends, and self-care. A layoff may even be a gift of time for things more important than work. You may have heard it said that on one's deathbed, we don't say we wish we spent more time with work.

Looking at the past brings regret and looking at the future brings worry. The only time that is real is the present moment. Accept it. Make the most of it. Be fully present whether with friends or family or in your job search. Take a breath and trust your time will come.

I accept the present moment and will make the most of it.

"*It is an equal failing to trust everybody, and to trust nobody.*"

English Proverb

TRUST

A job search can challenge our trust in ourselves and others. Sometimes the people we think will be our best supports are too discouraging or advice-giving when we may simply be looking for a listening ear.

When the going gets tough we may start to lose trust in ourselves. We may begin to doubt our dreams or have a hard time remembering successes from the past.

Since this is a vulnerable time, be selective in whom you choose for your inner circle. You may even need to put some distance between you and some well-meaning folks. When you start to lose faith and trust in your strengths, remind yourself of previous accomplishments. Trusted inner circle people can help you remember some of your strengths if you ask. People can also help with perspective, letting you know if you are too off track.

I trust that I know myself well
and also know in whom
to confide.

"Uncertainty is the only certainty there is, and knowing how to live with insecurity is the only security."

John Allen Paulos

UNCERTAINTY

So many unknowns can create negative emotions during your job search, such as waiting to hear back on an email or after an interview. There will be unexpected questions during an interview for which you can't prepare. When you do get an offer, you may wonder whether to accept it or whether you'll hit a land mine once there.

The reality is that life is filled with uncertainty, even when you have a job. Managing uncertainty is important so you don't get lost in feelings of fear and speculation.

Focus on what you can control, such as your schedule and job search efforts. Keeping busy, whether with a class or house project can divert your mind from worry. If your mind goes into a negative "what if" spin, remind yourself, "I can't possibly predict the future." Another strategy is defensive pessimism; this is increasing your confidence with coping by imaging a worst-case scenario and planning for it, such as making peace with an option to downsize your home. Mindfulness and stress reduction are additional strategies. You can choose to let uncertainty keep you up at night or see it as a challenge for practicing acceptance.

I accept uncertainty as part of life and find ways to cope.

"Each of us is a unique strand in the intricate web of life and here to make a contribution."

Deepak Chopra

UNIQUE

A job search is a time to reflect on what makes you unique. Reflection can help during the interview process or even beforehand when clarifying goals and job targets.

Sometimes all we want is a job, and it seems unrealistic to focus on our desires and uniqueness. Yet that quirky quality may be just the right fit for a job or employer.

Maybe you have a hard time even thinking about what makes you unique. Some take for granted a trait or skill because it is so natural. Consider asking three trusted family members or friends what unique or strong qualities they see in you. If you feel awkward, tell them it is a job search research project. You may be pleasantly surprised and get a needed boost to your confidence. Then think about how you can use that to serve society or your employer. Plus you will have more material for your resume, cover letters, and interviews.

I mine and remember my unique
traits and talents.

"When your values are clear to you, making decisions becomes easier."

Roy E. Disney

VALUES

What is important to you in your career and your life? This question about values is an important one to reflect on to keep perspective and also to stay grounded.

Of course, finding a career or job may be important at some level, even if out of financial necessity. Hopefully your role can also provide some sense of meaning or feeling of productivity in society. Remember your job is not your identity, so focusing on the other things you value in life can help keep perspective: family, friends, spirituality, community, hobbies, or a beloved pet.

Reflect also on what you value and want in a job. Values are as important as having your interests and strengths match the job. For example, are you motivated by meaning, money, adventure, or advancement? Priorities are different for everyone. Stay grounded in what you want so as not to be overly influenced by society or those around you.

I identify and stay grounded in
what is important in my life.

"When you visualize, then you materialize."

Denis Waitley

VISUALIZATION

Athletes and musicians use visualization to reach peak performance. Patients use visualization to enhance healing. You can use this strategy to increase job search success. Practical uses of visualization in the job search are to calm anxiety before an interview and to increase success by mentally rehearsing positive scenes.

Visualization is a cognitive tool, tapping imagination to realize an outcome. The strategy is based on the premise that the subconscious is programmable; it will look for and guide you to what you tell it.

A typical technique is to mentally imagine an event, such as a successful interview. See yourself vividly and specifically shaking hands, smiling, and answering questions calmly, competently, and confidently. Visualize receiving the phone call with the job offer of your dreams and feel the excitement. Feel the experience in the present as if it is actually happening. Reduce anxiety before an interview, phone call, or networking meeting by visualizing a calm place or looking at a soothing picture. The mind is a powerful tool that can create success and happiness.

I tap my mind to visualize
a positive outcome.

"Early to bed and early to rise, makes a man healthy, wealthy, and wise."

Benjamin Franklin

WELLNESS

A job search can take its toll emotionally and physically. When discouraged, it's all too easy to reach for that chocolate bar, glass of wine, or pillow, yet this is when you most need to eat healthily, exercise regularly, and get a good night's sleep. Not taking care of yourself can decrease energy and self-image, which may come across in networking meetings and interviews.

Self-care is also enjoying personal time to avoid burnout. Walks in the park, crossword puzzles, and visits to supportive friends and family are affordable, even if you're unemployed.

Call a friend, put on those athletic shoes, and get some fresh air. When you come back, maybe make a colorful, healthy salad, draw water for a soothing bath, read an inspirational book and get a good night's sleep. Wake up with an affirmation or prayer for a fresh start.

I take care of myself
to be healthy and successful
in the job search.

"Wisdom is not a product of schooling, but of the lifelong attempt to acquire it."

Albert Einstein

WISDOM

Sometimes you may feel like you are losing your inner compass as you navigate the job search. Your world can feel upside down. Rejections and lack of response can cause your confidence to plummet. Go deeper to mine your wisdom, which may be buried in the depths of despair.

Many sources of wisdom can be helpful. Sometimes you may seek guidance from family, friends, and colleagues regarding career choices and job search strategy. Opinions are based on individual experiences and values, so you need to see what fits. Sometimes you may seek advice from professionals or career reading. Outside sources are good for their objectivity, yet can vary widely and be confusing.

In the end, wisdom emerges from many sources. Invite forth your inner wisdom. Sit in silence. Pray. Meditate. Reflect. Wait, listen, and then honor what comes forth.

> I listen for and honor
> my own wisdom.

*"If you've got it,
you've got it, and it
doesn't matter how
old you are."*

Simon Cowell

X-FACTOR

You had all the right qualifications, were sure this job was made for you, but you didn't get it. Worse yet, you learned someone with fewer qualifications was hired.

Sometimes the hired person gets a breakthrough while networking. Sometimes they are chosen for the x-factor, an attribute or quality beyond description. Although the x-factor can refer to an extraordinary quality, it can also simply be that indefinable something that even makes an employer overlook qualities that are negative or missing.

While there is no way to create an x-factor, choosing job targets and prospective employers that are superb matches will increase your chances. Then trust that an opportunity will unfold for which you are uniquely qualified, quirks and all.

I accept the mystery of the job search and trust that the right fit will come.

"You are now at a crossroads. Forget your past. Who are you now?"

Anthony Robbins

X-ROADS

Your job search may present a career crossroads, whether this search is your choice or you lost your job. Now could be an opportunity to say to yourself that you deserve career happiness and satisfaction. Now may be the time to take that risk you have been thinking about.

Life is too short to be resigned and feel there is no other choice. Understandably, life may have some constraints, whether it be a mortgage, child rearing costs, or retraining. Sometimes we have more choices than we allow ourselves to consider. Sometimes our barriers to explore meaning and happiness are internal fears and perspectives.

Consider paths on the crossroads that may not be on the typical main road. Consider devoting 25 percent of your career search time to explore a dream or to think about it as a longer-range goal.

I allow myself to consider the opportunities of this crossroad.

"Cynics always say no. But saying 'yes' begins things. Saying 'yes' is how things grow. Saying 'yes' leads to knowledge."

Stephen Colbert

YES

You are waiting for the job offer to say "yes" to. In the meantime, say "yes" to other opportunities. Sometimes "yes" is the last word you want to say when someone suggests an idea, job lead, or networking contact. Advice can be tiring. While it is good to have clear goals and a plan, maybe the new angle will bring a new result.

Balance saying "yes" with discernment. Honor your inner wisdom, yet be on alert that fear and procrastination can keep you from moving forward.

The networking event may be more fun than you think, the job lead may not be too much of a stretch, or the contact may introduce you to a better connection. Saying "yes" may shift the outcome and your energy.

I try new angles and welcome
new experiences.

"When you expect things to happen – strangely enough – they do happen."

J.P.Morgan

YET

Hearing the question, "Did you find a job yet?" can make a person cringe. Rather than stammer or give a rundown of all your efforts, reclaim the word "yet." The phrase "not yet" means it's just a matter of time. Owning the expectation that success will occur in the future can give you a sense of hope rather than feeling stuck in current circumstances.

Before others ask, consider proactively sharing, "In case you're wondering, I didn't get my dream job yet." Instead of thinking or saying, "I'm not getting anywhere with networking," say "Networking hasn't paid off yet." Instead of, "I'm not hearing back," think, "I've not heard back yet." A slightly more hopeful perspective may help you reframe and regain a more positive attitude that can help your job search.

The next time someone asks you if you've gotten a job, hold your head up high and say, "Not yet, but there's always tomorrow."

I remember that "yet" holds hope for the future.

"Experience shows that success is due less to ability than to zeal. The winner is he who gives himself to his work, body and soul."

Sir Thomas Fowell Buxton

ZEAL

The idea of having zeal for a job may seem out of reach. Having zeal in a job search may seem even more unlikely. Both situations can be positive aspirations for you and also what an employer looks for.

Though you may feel like you "just need to get a job," you can take this as an opportunity to explore more career happiness, if not passion. Think of a time you had natural enthusiasm and energy. Look to that situation for clues to a career choice or employer target. If now is not the time to explore a career passion, then bring those interests into your personal life to create energy for your job search or happiness in your life.

Try to positively motivate yourself in the search rather than be gripped by fear or pessimism. One motivation may be to get a job to support your family or retirement. Find something about the employer to get excited about, whether it's the service or a product or the employer's values. When you are in the job, find a niche where you can express your zeal, whether it's helping a stressed customer, solving a complex problem, or volunteering for a special project.

I uncover and express zeal for something in my life.

"Intelligence is the ability to adapt to change."

Stephen Hawking

ZIGZAG

Career paths aren't a straight line in today's unpredictable world. Your job search may also feel like it zigzags, pulling you along for the ride.

You may have been laid off due to a shift in your industry or a sharp downturn in company profits. You may need to shift your career based on the job market. With the job search itself, you may feel the zigzag with positive responses on some days and negative responses on others.

Cope by realizing that fluctuations in a career or job search are normal and natural. Focus on wondering if something better might be around the next bend. Try a new angle in your strategy. Once in a new job, continually develop new skills to be ahead of the curve.

I respond to unexpected turns with grace and curiosity.

BEST WISHES ON YOUR JOURNEY

I hope these pages brought you some comfort as you navigate the emotional ups and downs of the job search. By normalizing challenging feelings, you can remember that you are not alone. Try not to be too hard on yourself.

Equally or more importantly, I hope this book reminds you of the power of your thoughts. What you think and say to yourself affects your feelings and behavior. Reframing negative self-talk will help you be more successful in your job search. This skill can also help you have more success and happiness in life.

May the strategies of using affirmations (whether believable or more optimistic) enable you to align your feelings and job search in a positive direction. If you need more assistance to survive and thrive, please consider the services of a career counselor or therapist.

A final affirmation:

I am gentle with myself while also taking steps to stay positive on this journey.

ABOUT KAREN

Karen Litzinger, MA, LPC is a career counselor, professional speaker, and obsessive fan of daily inspiration books. She has coached thousands of clients, including through twenty years in her own business, Litzinger Career Consulting. Karen is a Licensed Professional Counselor and Certified Career Counselor. She lives in Pittsburgh, PA, where she leads a neighborhood Block Watch, coordinates a school sponsorship in India, and delights in her dog, Georgie. You can find more about Karen at KarensCareerCoaching.com.

CPSIA information can be obtained
at www.ICGtesting.com
Printed in the USA
BVHW050442011221
622871BV00018B/803

9 781737 760009